AF430321

SEEDS OF FAITH

A 31-DAY DEVOTIONAL

If you have faith as a mustard seed, you will say to this mountain, 'Move from here to there,' and it will move; and nothing will be impossible for you. —Jesus in Matthew 17:20

Contents

To my three beautiful children Kavaughn, Kayden and Kasey. I love you more than words can express. I know I have made some mistakes along the way and for that I'm sorry. Please know my mistakes came from a lack of understanding but never from a lack of love. Remember to always walk boldly and confidently with your head healed high for God who is our guide walks right by your side. Never ever doubt for a second that you CAN! Do whatever you set your mind too! Always remember I love you more, but God loves you BEST!

About the Author

Precious Downey was born March 25, 1979 in East Cleveland, Ohio to Jake and Callie Thomas. Both of my parents were devoted Christians and raised my sibling and I accordingly. The youngest of three siblings, we grew up knowing the importance of committing our hearts to the Lord.

I was raised in the inner city of East Cleveland where I saw poverty and lack. Yet, I always knew I wanted "better" out of life but not fully knowing how to achieve better. After graduating from Shaw High School in 1997, I became a young mother at the age of 18 and married by the age of 20. During that time in my life it was extremely difficult, because my peers where going off to college and figuring out the plans for their future. I was navigating through life hardships such as working a full time job, putting food on the table, paying bills, and taking care of my family.

Because of my faith in God I decided not to feel sorry for myself, and made a decision to push forward in life regardless of how difficult my life was at that time. Although life was far from easy, my difficult circumstances allowed God's persistent love for me to show up in new ways.

When I finally decided to forgive myself for getting pregnant at 18, I began to believe that I was still worthy of God's best! I was finally able to walk in total forgiveness and freedom. I began to believe I deserved everything good God had in store for me.

Today, I'm a college graduate, with three beautiful children, and a first time author and writer. I hope my story of self-forgiveness, hard work and determination inspires those with similar stories to never quit, keep trusting and believing that God has prepared great things in store for those who love him (Jeremiah 29:11).

See her website: www.preciousdowney.com or scan the QR code for quick access on your phone or tablet.

Before You Read

Father God, I ask that you touch the mind of the person reading this book right now. Open their hearts and minds to hear from you. Allow the Holy Spirit to take up permanent residence in their life. Show them that you are God and God alone! There is no other beside you! You are the beginning and the end. You are greater than every principality, spiritual wickedness, Satanic opposition and every stronghold from the enemy. May Your spirit of victory and truth dwell in the deepest part of their soul and remind them they were born to be a citizen of your mighty Kingdom.

31 Daily Devotionals

Reach

Lord, help me to forget all that is behind me so that I can reach forward to the future and grab what you have ahead for me. Help me to raise above fear and doubt. When life gets overwhelming, remind me that you are greater than anything that I face. Even when the situation is too much for me, it's not too much for you. Allow me to be totally dependent on you and the will you have for my life.

Forgetting those things which are behind, and reaching forth unto those things which are before, I press toward the mark for the prize of the high calling of God in Christ Jesus. —Philippians 3:13-14

Close

Lord, I don't want anything to come between You and I. Help me to hear your voice clearly and obey your Word so I can live a life that is pleasing to you. Please remove anything that keeps me from a closer walk with you. Guide me in a plain path of righteousness according to your will and glory. Shape me, mold me, use me and fill me each and everyday to become more like you. Thank you that I can cast all of my worries and anxieties upon you because you care for me. Lord, thank you that for whatever I ask in your name, you will do so that God the Father may be glorified in you.

But your iniquities have made a separation between you and your God, and your sins have hidden his face from you so that he does not hear.
—Isaiah 59:2

Peace & Joy

Lord, whenever grief, sadness or depression tries to come and torture me, I ask that you give me your peace that surpasses all understanding. I pour out my worries, fears and anxieties at your feet. I'm declaring your promises for blessings of peace, joy and strength over my life. Allow me to understand that no matter what life throws at me, I can have peace and joy knowing that my victory lies in you and not in my circumstances.

Blessed are those who mourn, for they shall be comforted.
—Matthew 5:4

Fill Me

Father God, remove all confusion, depression anxiety, fear and uncertainity out of my life. Fill me with your unweaving love, peace and calmness. Help me to focus on your Word and your promises for my life. Fill my heart with an insight of your goodness that will redirect me on the path towards your truth and light. Help me to not focus on my circumstances but stand firm on your unwavering promises.

Set your mind on things above not on things on the earth.
—*Colossians 3:2*

No Weapon

Father God, I thank you that no matter what mountain we come up against you go before me making my crooked path straight. Lord, I thank you that no weapon the enemy tries to use against me shall prosper. I pray that you shield me from harm and danger. Cover me in your entire armor. I put on the helmet of salvation, the breastplate of righteousness , the belt of truth, the boots of peace. I'm always ready to face each day because your light surrounds me, your love enfolds me, and your presence protects me. Your righteousness in my life protects me from things that are sent to destroy me. I already have the victory!

So do not fear, for I am with you; do not be dismayed, for I am your God. I will strengthen you and help you; I will uphold you with my righteous right hand. —Isaiah 41;10

Protector

Lord, thank you that I can run to you as my protector and my refuge in times of trouble. When life gets hard help me to remember that you are with me and I am never alone. May I dwell in the safety of your loving arms. Please protect me physically, mentally, spiritually in any and every way possible. Let your angels fight against any demonic forces that may come against me today. May all the plans of the enemy come to nothing in our lives. I cannot live without you. I'm able to face trials because I know you are here with me. Allow me to feel your protection and presence wherever I go.

Fear not, for I am with you; be not dismayed, for I am your God; I will strengthen you, I will help you, I will uphold you with my righteous right hand. —Isaiah 41:10

Ready for Romance?

Father God, before I become romantically involved with another person, help me to become emotionally healthy and grounded in love and authenticy. Help me to grow and develop so that I can give and receive love without my personal issues getting in the way. May your Holy Spirit guide me in dealing with my insecurities. Allow me to learn appropriate ways for conflict resolution and show me what healthy communication skills are in a loving, God fearing relationship. Help me to find a partner who brings enhancement to me in his/her very being—brings more love, joy, peace and prosperity to my life. A partner I can love fully and who can fully receive my love. May my heart be open and my head be clear.

But from the beginning of creation God made them male and female. For this cause shall a man leaves his father and mother and cleave to his wife and they twain shall be one flesh so then they are no more twain, but one flesh. —Mark 10:6-9

In Christ

Father God, help me to understand fully who I am in Christ. Help me to understand that everything wonderful about me is only because I am made by you who creates wonderful works. Thank you for setting me apart and knowing me before I was formed in my mother's womb. I thank you that your Word gives knowledge, instruction, wisdom and understanding to all who pay attention to its truth. Help me to use the gifts you have given me in a mighty way that glories your precious name. Thank you for creating me in your perfect image.

Each of you should use whatever gift you have received to serve others, as faithful stewards of God's grace in its various forms.
—1 Peter 4:10

Fearless

Lord, sometimes I am afraid of what might happen in the future. Help me to defeat the spirit of fear and allow me to experience your peace that surpasses all understanding. When I am afraid, God help me to place my faith and trust in you. Help me to remember that I never have to be afraid or live in fear. Thank you God that you are always on my side and will fight for me during my darkest times. When you are on my side no darkness can ever succeed against me.

Be strong and of good courage, do not fear nor be afraid of them for the lord your God, He is the one who goes with you. He will not leave you nor forsake you. —Deuteronomy 31:6

Wonderfully Made

Father God, help me to understand fully who I am in Christ. Help me to understand that everything wonderful about me is only because of who you are. Contrary to what people or science might tell me, I'm not the result of random cosmic collisons but was knit together by you in my mother's womb. I have been created with love, dignity and purpose. When the world tells me that I'm defined by my struggles, accomplishments or appearance, help me to hide in you God who are the author of my life and the source of my true identity and worth. Help me to use the gifts you have given me in a mighty way that glories your precious name. Thank you for creating me in your perfect image.

I will praise You, for I am fearfully and wonderfully made; Marvelous are Your works, and that my soul knows very well.
—Psalms 139:14

Elevating Above Depression

Holy Spirit, you are my Comforter and I ask that you comfort my heart at this time. I ask that you strengthen me where I feel weak and whisper words of confidence and encouragement to the deepest part of my soul. I ask that you would send me your warring angels to bind the spirit of depression, anxiety, and evilness that surrounds me. Fill my mind with your wisdom and enlightenment to see a way out of this state of depression. Close every door that I have left open to demonic spirits due to my own negligence. Give me the gift of discernment so when the spirit of depression comes in I can bind it up before it attacks. Send your ministering angels to speak life, truth, and hope over my life. Help me to remember no weapons that are ever formed against me shall prosper and I know that I shall live a life of peace, joy, and happiness. Fill me from the top of my head to the tip of my toes with your Holy Spirit.

Come to Me, all you who labor and are heavy laden, and I will give you rest. Take My yoke upon you and learn from Me, for I am gentle and lowly in heart, and you will find rest for your souls. —Matthew 11:28-29

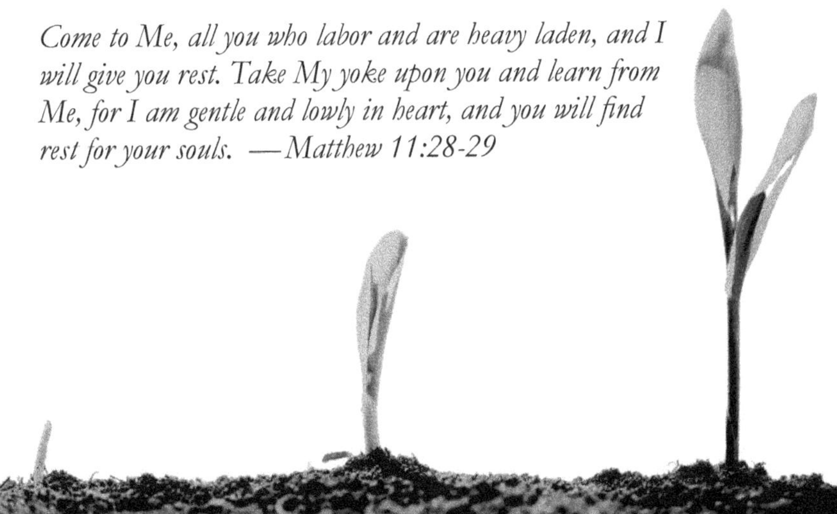

Devoted

Lord, help me to remember that giving devotion to anything or anyone on earth means it is destined for decay, death or destruction. I ask Lord that all the connections in my life that are not apart of your plan for me would be revealed in your name, Jesus. Help me to remember that only the things we do for the kingdom will last forever. Keep me free from idolizing money and the material possessions of the world. Help me to set my mind on things that are above and not on things that are on earth.

Do not love the world or the things in the world. If anyone loves the world , the love of the father is not in them. For all things of the world—the desire of the flesh and the desires of the eye and pride posessions—is not from the father but is from the world. And the world is passing away with its desires but whoever does the will of God abides forever. —1 John 2:15-17

A Plan for My Future

Father God, I come before you today and I know that you love me and that you have a plan for my future. A plan of hope and goodness because you are a good God. As I wait expectantly and patiently upon you, may I never envy a sinner. May I never become jealous of how you are blessing others around me because I know that I'm next and my time is coming! Even though things may not look the way I want them to in the natural. I know I serve a supernatural God and I belive you have a beautiful reward for me. Allow my hope, expectation, and patience grow more and more each day as I look to you for guidance and reassurance.

Do not let your heart envy sinners, but be zealous for the fear of the LORD all the day; For surely there is a hereafter, and your hope will not be cut off. — Proverbs 23:17-18

Like You

Lord, help me to be more like you. Fill me with your grace, mercy and compassion so that I will be able to extend those to others. Help me to be gracious, loving and full of compassion to everyone I meet. Keep me from any kind of emotional outburst or reactions to things that are inspired by my flesh and that are displeasing to you. In all situations help me to remember that life and death are in the power of the tongue, therefore help me to be a person full of loving and kind words. Allow your Holy Spirit to fill me with your love, peace, patience, compassion and self control. I always want to reflect a spirit of kindness and gentleness with every person I meet. I want to be a reflection of your goodness.

Death and life are in the power of the tongue, And those who love it will eat its fruit. Proverbs 18:21

Abundant Father

Father God, thankyou that you are the giver of good gifts and it is your desire to lavish me with your goodness, favor and your grace. Forgive me for the many times I remained stuck in a poverty mindset for you are a God of overflow. I reject the lies from the enemy that I will forever be in debt, depleting wants or needs. I destroy all the lies of the enemy that tells me that my life of financial problems is what I deserve and will always be. I believe the truth that you died to give me an abundant life and you will supply all of my needs. I will walk, talk and live a lifestyle as a child of a king for you are head over my life and my finances.

And you shall remember the Lord your God, for it is He who gives you power to get wealth, that He may establish His covenant which He swore to your fathers, as it is this day. —Deuteronomy 8:18

Centered

Lord, often times I feel stressed and overwhelmed with an intense pressure from my job. Father God, quiet my emotions and center my thoughts so I can perform my job successfully. In these moments of worry, help me remember you are my rock and in you there is no fear or anxiety. Help me respond to my problems by giving thanks in the midst of uncertainty. Lord grant me your grace to excel in my career. Remind me Father God that you have not given me a spirit of fear or anxiety, but of power and a sound mind. Help me to remember that your power is made perfect in my weakness. It is my desire to represent your character and nature well in my workplace.

Whatever you do work heartily, as for the Lord and not for men, knowing that from the Lord you will receive the inheritance as your reward. You are serving the Lord Jesus Christ.
— Colossians 3:23-24

Sweet Release

Father God, help me to release past hurts, resentment and anger towards people who have hurt and betrayed me. Only you know father God how deep the hurt goes and how long I have lived with this agony. Father God take away the heavy burden of unforgiveness and bitterness that consumes me. Help me to demonstrate unconditional love and compassion for myself and those who have hurt me. Allow your Holy Spirit to fill me with your peace and help me to choose forgiveness in the same way you have forgiven me.

When you Stand praying, if you hold anything against anyone, forgive them, so that your father in heaven may forgive your sins.
—Mark 11:25

Total Wellness

Father God, I thankyou that you are the only source for health and healing. When I'am overwhelmed with health problems help me to remember your supernatural power and strength flows within me. Help me to never give up on myself but allow me to rest in your promises. When the pain and hurt is overwhelming help me to see the good and blessing that surrounds me every day. I thank you that you are a God of the impossible. I believe that by your stripes, Lord Jesus, I am healed and will continue to walk by faith and not by sight. There is nothing you can't do! I ask for your complete and total healing of everything that is disruptive in my mind and body. I trust that you will restore me and raise me up to complete health.

But I will restore you to health and heal your wounds, declares the Lord. —Jeremiah 30:17

Worship the Lord your God and his blessing will be on your food and water. I will take away sinckness from among you. —Exodus 23: 25

My Children

Father God, help me to become a better parent. Forgive me for the mistakes I made out of my own unresolved hurts, traumas and selfishness. Fill me with your goodness and mercy, that it may overflow into my children. Teach me to understand my children and to listen without judgement, and harshness but to always respond from a place of love, understanding and patience. Help me to be courteous to them as I want them to be courteous to me. I need your wisdom and strength to train them in the way they should go. I pray that my children will never be conformed to the world, but instead, inspire them to seek first your kingdom and righteousness. Protect them, Lord, from the schemes of the enemy and from every demonic influence of the world that seeks to turn their hearts away from you.

Children are a gift from the Lord. —Psalm 127:3

Jesus said, "Let the little children come to me and do not hinder them, for the kindom of heaven belongs to such as these." —Matthew 19:14

Train up a child in the way he should go and when he is old he will not depart from it. — Proverb 22:6

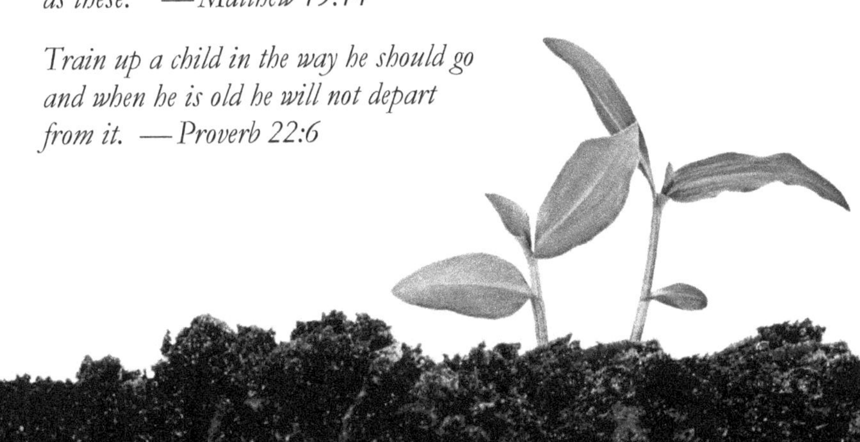

Power of Christ

Father God, I always want to be a follower and disciple of you. But at times I'm scared and weak because of hardships, insults and persecutions. Sometimes the persecutions and burdens are so heavy, it is too difficult for me to carry. Help me to remember my burdens are not mine to carry but it is necessary for me to release my burdens upon you. Remind me that your grace is sufficient and it is made perfect in my weakness. For when I'am weak, you are strong. Teach me to delight and boast in my infirmities for the power of Christ may rest upon me forever.

Come to me, all you who are weary and burdened, and I will give you rest. Take my yoke upon you and learn from me, for I am gentle and humble in heart, and you will find rest for your souls. For my yoke is easy and my burden is light. —Matthew 11:28–30

My Marriage

Father God, I extend my marriage to you. I pray our marriage will bring you glory and honor ... Give us both the patience, compassion and understanding to be united in love and to handle our emotions wisely. Help us to look for the good in each other and overlook any perceived flaws. Help us to love each other even when its difficult to like each other. When we disagree, Father God, help us to approach one another with humility and respect. Allow us to always keep a united front for each other letting nothing or no one come in-between us. Allow your healing hands to be upon us and remove all unforgiveness, bitterness and sadness from our hearts. Help us to be of one spirit and one mind and to value each other above ourselves.

Whatever you do work heartily, as for the Lord and not for men, knowing that from the Lord you will receive the inheritance as your reward. You are serving the Lord Jesus Christ. — Colossians 3:23-24

Therefore a man shall leave his father and his mother and hold fast to his wife, they shall become one fleesh. — Genesis 2: 24

Bear with each other and forgive one another if any of you has a grievance against someone. Forgive as the Lord forgave you.
— Colossians 3:13

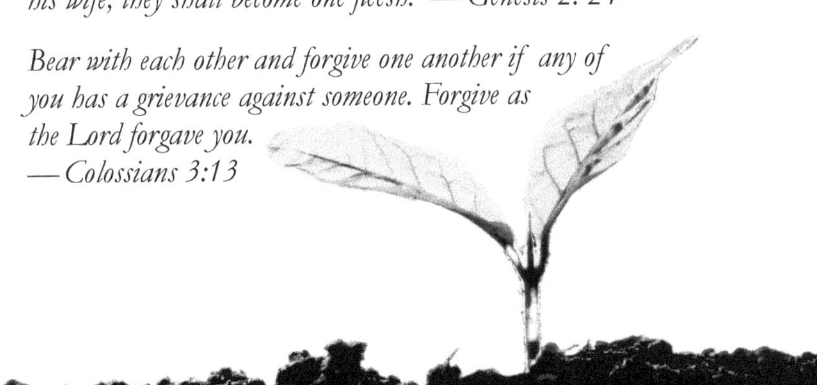

My Husband

Father God, I pray that you will help my husband stand strong against temptation. Protect his mind from the influences of the world. Help him to not seek the validation and lies of the world, for it is foolishness to you. I pray that he will listen and obey your teaching and follow your commandments wholeheartly so he can stand strongly and boldly against the temptations from the enemy. Help him to grow in wisdom and in truth through your Word. Help him to not waiver to the right or the left but to stay focused and fixed on you. Each day, allow him to grow in his faith and become the man of God you are calling him to be. Surround him with Godly men of faith who will hold him accountable, who will reference your Word, who will encourage, uplift and most importantly challenge him to be a Stuart man of God.

Wives, submit yourselves to your own husbands as you do to the Lord.
—Ephesisans 5:22

Turn my eyes away from worthless things; preserve my life according to Your Word. —Psalms 119:37

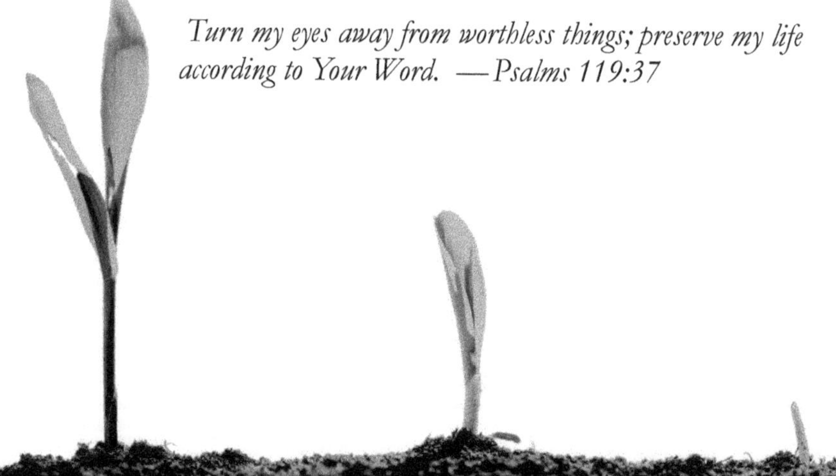

New Beginnings

Father God, thank you for never leaving me or forsaking me. I thank you because you are a God of new beginnings and endings. As I embrack on a new journey in my life. I ask that you order my steps and direct my path. Father God Give me the strength and courage I need to pursue this new chapter in my life with grace and a understanding that you are right here with me. Remove all fear and anxiety for I know you are making a way in the wilderness and streams in the wasteland. For I know you are not a God of confusion but a God of clarity and a sound mind.

Behold the former things have come to pass and new things do I declare before they spring forth I tell you of them. —Isiah 42:9

For the know the plans I have for you. Declares the Lord plans to prosper you and not harm you plans to give you hope for the future. —Jeremiah 29:11

Souls

Father God, I pray for lost souls. Bless those souls who don't know who you are, and who have harden their heart against you. I pray for anyone who is convicted by the world that God isn't true or doesn't exist. God please remove the evil influences from their lives that are blocking them from having a relationship with you. Uproot every lie that has been planted by the enemy and be exposed by the Word of God. Lord open up the hearts of those who are lost that they may be able to hear the Word and accept it as the one and only TRUTH! Replace their hardened hearts with a new heart that is filled with your love and compassion. I pray that your love touches the deepest part of their soul and that your Word transform their lives.

But even if our gospel is veiled, it is veiled to those who are perishing, whose minds the god of this age has blinded, who do not believe, lest the light of the gospel of the glory of Christ, who is the image of God, should shine on them. —2 Corinthians 4:3-4

Praying for Wisdom

Thank you, God that you know my heart. You understand my deepest wants and needs, and you know my every intention. You know me better than I know myself. There is nowhere I could run to escape your presence, and nothing I could hide from you! And that's why right now, I'm asking you to give me your divine wisdom and guidance. I often worry about making the right decision, but I want to live a life that honors you. Guide me, Father God, and show me the paths that lead to abundant life and convict me when I am tempted to stray away from you. Hold me close and teach me to walk in a manner worthy of the calling you have given me. Direct my steps as you guard my life because I want to live a life that glorifies your name.

Likewise the Spirit also helps in our weaknesses. For we do not know what we should pray for as we ought, but the Spirit Himself makes intercession for us with groanings which cannot be uttered.
—Romans 8:26

Simply Thank You

Father God, I come before you today not to ask you for anything but to simply say thank you. What a privilege it is to wake up and be alive! Father God, I thank you that you are able to bring hope and light even through the darkest moments of my life. Father, I thank you for never giving up on me during times I wanted to give up on myself. I thank you for your love and strength that you give to me each any every day. Because of you, Father God, I'm more than a conqueror and I am destined to win simply because of who you are. Thank you for creating me in your perfect image and likeness, no less than anyone else but an original by your design. My heart is overwhelmingly grateful as it overflows with love and gratitude. I will forever give you praise and bless your holy name.

I will give thanks to you Lord, with all my heart. I will tell of all your wonderful deeds." —Palsm 9:1

Source

Father God, help me to remember that my job is not my source, but you are my source and my provider. Although my works are committed to you lord often times my job leaves me emotionally drained and unfulfilled. Help me to remember that sometimes the blessings are in not what you give but in what you take away. Father God, I have faith right now that you are opening the right doors, closing the wrong doors and lining up the right breaks and opportunity for my life. I turn to you seeking your divine help and guidance as I look for suitable employment that brings fulfillment, peace inspiration and purpose.

Whatever you do, work at it with all your heart as working or the lord not for human masters, since you know that you will receive and inheritance from the Lord as a reward. It is the Lord Crist you are serving. — Colossians 3:23-24

Wholeness & Deliverance

Thank you for the sacrifice of your son, Jesus. His death gave me eternal life so every single one of my transgressions past, present and future was nailed upon him when he died on the cross. His death brought wholeness to my mind, body, soul and spirit. His death brought me a complete and total deliverance. Because I'm your child I have received the healing I so graciously need through the divine connection of the Holy Spirit. Allow your Holy Spirit to guide me each and everyday so that I can make the right choices and live a life of complete and total freedom.

He was wounded for our transgressions, he was bruised for our iniquities; the chastisement of our peace was upon him and with his stripes we are healed. —Isaiah 53:5

Mend Me

Father God, I'am having a difficult time dealing with the passing of my mother. My heart is completely broken, and this heaviness is too difficult for me to carry. Where I was once filled with certainty and clarity, I now feel lost, alone and confused. I do not know where to go from here. I know my mother would not want me to dwell so much on this pain but be thankful for all the memories we once shared. Father God, wrap me in your loving arms and provide me with your profound healing. Begin to mend the pieces of my broken heart for I know broken hearts are made whole in your hands.

Come to me, all who labor and are weary and heavy burdened , and I will give you rest. Take my yoke upon you and learn from me, for I am gentle and humble in heart and you will find rest for your souls. For my yoke is easy and my burden is light. —Matthew 11:28-30

Perfect Father God

Lord, I am so overwhelmed by the loss of my father. I am deeply hurt and My heart is full with sorrow. I know that he is with you in heaven but the loss is still so great to bear. I find it extremely hard to concentrate and move throughout my day. I can't bear the thought of living in this world without my father. My world is completely shattered. Remind me that you are a perfect God who makes no mistakes and I am never alone no matter what is taking place. I pray that your divine comfort reaches my heart and fills me with your love and peace that surpasses all understanding.

Do not let your hearts be troubled. You believe in God; believe also in me. My Father's house has many rooms; if that were not so, would I have told you that I am going there to prepare a place for you? And if I go and prepare a place for you, I will come back and take you to be with me that you also may be where I am. You know the way to the place where I am going. —John 14: 1-27

Walk with Me

Father God, I praise and glorify your holy name. I thank you for the promises and hope of your Word. Thank you for your guidance and your divine protection. Continue to walk with me each and everyday. Allow your Word and truth to minister to my heart and soul. Turn my heart away from sin and renew my mind to seek your goodness, faithfulness, and truth in every situation. Show me your ways so I can walk securely even in the face of darkness and adversity. Give me the free gift of your Holy Spirit so that I may live a life that honors you. Give me the strength and wisdom I need to learn your ways so that I might follow you as my Lord and Savior. My hope and faith are in you all the days of my life.

For we walk by faith and not by sight. —*2 Cornithaians 5:7*

Extraordinary Quotes on Prayer

"It would be of course a low voltage spiritual life in which prayer was chiefly undertaken as a discipline, rather than as a way of co-laboring with God to accomplish good things and advancing his Kingdom purposes." — Dallas Willard

"Unless in the first waking moment of the day you learn to fling the door wide back and let God in, you will work on a wrong level all day; but swing the door wide open and pray to your Father in secret, and every public thing will be stamped with the presence of God."
— Oswald Chambers

"Prayers outlive the lives of those who uttered them; outlive a generation, outlive an age, outlive a world." — E.M. Bounds

"Our prayers lay the track down which God's power can come. Like a mighty locomotive, his power is irresistible, but it cannot reach us without rails." — Watchman Nee

"I saw more clearly than ever, that the first great and primary business to which I ought to attend every day was, to have my soul happy in the Lord." — George Mueller

"God does nothing but by prayer, and everything with it."
— John Wesley

"But when we pray, genuinely pray, the real condition of our heart is revealed. This is as it should be. This is when God truly begins to work with us. The adventure is just beginning." — Richard Foster

Extraordinary Quotes on Prayer

"Effective prayer is prayer that attains what it seeks. It is prayer that moves God, effecting its end." — Charles G. Finney

"Mind how you pray. Make real business of it. Let it never be a dead formality ... plead the promise in a truthful, business-like way ... Ask for what you want, because the Lord has promised it. Believe that you have the blessing, and go forth to your work in full assurance of it. Go from your knees singing, because the promise is fulfilled ...."
— C.H. Spurgeon

"All that God is, and all that God has, is at the disposal of prayer. But we must use the key. Prayer can do anything that God can do, and as God can do anything, prayer is omnipotent." — R.A. Torrey

"Relying on God has to begin all over again every day as if nothing had yet been done." — C.S. Lewis

"Prayer is not overcoming God's reluctance, but laying hold of His willingness." — Martin Luther

"Prayer is the open admission that without Christ we can do nothing. And prayer is the turning away from ourselves to God in the confidence that He will provide the help we need. Prayer humbles us as needy and exalts God as wealthy." — John Piper

Personal Notes

Personal Notes

Personal Notes

Personal Notes